D0602999

Hearth & Home

Christmas *Customs*

Hearth & Home

CREATIVE
PUBLISHING
international

MINNETONKA, MINNESOTA

Copyright © 2001
Creative Publishing international, Inc.
5900 Green Oak Drive
Minnetonka, Minnesota 55343
1-800-328-3895
All rights reserved.
www.howtobookstore.com

President/CEO: David D. Murphy

CHRISTMAS CUSTOMS: HEARTH & HOME
Created by the editors of Creative Publishing international.

Executive Editor: Elaine Perry
Senior Editor: Linda Neubauer
Senior Art Director: Stephanie Michaud
Art Director: Mark Jacobson
Desktop Publishing Specialist: Laurie Kristensen
Project & Prop Stylist: Joanne Wawra
Samplemaker: Arlene Dohrman
Photographer: Tate Carlson
Director of Production Services: Kim Gerber

Creative Publishing international, Inc. offers a variety of how-to
books. For information write:
    Creative Publishing international, Inc.
        Subscriber Books
    5900 Green Oak Drive
    Minnetonka, MN 55343

Due to differing conditions, materials, and skill levels, the publisher
and various manufacturers disclaim any liability for unsatisfactory
results or injury due to improper use of tools, materials, or
information in this publication.

All rights reserved. No part of this publication may be reproduced,
stored in a retrieval system or transmitted in any form or by any
means, electronic, mechanical, photocopying, recording or
otherwise, without the prior written permission of the publisher.

ISBN 1-58923-012-4

Printed in Singapore
10 9 8 7 6 5 4 3 2 1

Table of Contents

Every year December brings with it a heightening sense of expectation for the coming Christmas. As we count off the days and plan for the celebration, we incorporate a few age-old customs that seemingly make the season more meaningful. So accustomed are we to these rituals, that often their origins and symbolism are overlooked or forgotten. We love our handcrafted Christmas stockings and we hang them from the mantel every year, never stopping to wonder where this tradition began. We bake Christmas cookies and send Christmas cards without a thought to the origin of such habits. We might circle round the Christmas tree singing carols or take a Christmas Eve drive down dark streets lit only with rows of glowing luminaria, knowing our ancestors did the same, but not knowing why. This book sheds light on the origins of some of these lovely traditions, hopefully making them a more meaningful expression of the Christmas spirit.

The Hearth

One of the dictionary definitions of "hearth" is "a vital or creative center." Another describes a hearth as synonymous with "family life" and "home." Little wonder, when once upon a time so much of the daily routine of life in every home centered around the fireplace: cooking food, washing clothes, reading stories by firelight, and staying warm. In our modern world there is little actual need for the fireplace. We cook food on kitchen stoves, wash clothes in well-equipped laundry rooms, flip electrical switches for light, and rely on furnaces run by automatic thermostats to keep us warm. The fireplace is ornamental at best, occasionally employed to add cozy atmosphere on a wintry night.

Yet at Christmastime, we turn our attention to the hearth. The mantel serves as a stage for our Christmas collectibles and the traditional hanging spot for our Christmas stockings. Stories are told by the crackling fire of how Santa will somehow descend down the chimney, bringing his bounty of gifts. Decked out with garlands of greenery, the hearth becomes a feast for the eyes and a vital center of Christmas customs in the home once more.

Mantel decorations can be simple or elaborate, playful or sophisticated. Here a pair of Santa's reindeer and clusters of candles in brass candlesticks are arranged on an ornate mantel with greenery, pinecones, and berries. The papier-mâché reindeer, gilded with metallic paint, are elegant accents for the intricate carving on the mantel.

Amaryllises are set on each side of a picture, dominating this Christmas display.

A countdown calendar decorates this mantel. It is made by hanging twenty-four stocking ornaments, filled with holiday candies, along a fresh garland. A star ornament hangs at the end of the garland for Christmas day.

How to make a Mantel Cloth

Assemble a mantel cloth from overlapping plaid napkins. Use the space to display a Nativity scene or a collection of Christmas artwork or memorabilia.

Materials

- Dinner napkins in plaids and solid colors.
- Double-stick tape.
- Small safety pins.
- Narrow wired ribbon.
- Medium-size jingle bells (or small ornaments).

1 Arrange napkins on the mantel with points hanging down. Overlap and adjust placement to cover the entire mantel. Pin the layers together temporarily. Secure with double-stick tape or safety pins, inserted from the underside. Turn under the napkins at the back of the mantel.

2 Tie a small wired ribbon bow for each napkin point. Hand-stitch a small bell or ornament and a bow to each point.

3 Secure the arrangement to the mantel, using double-stick tape.

Christmas Stockings

Santa Claus is much more than a myth. His character is most likely based on the true life of Nicholas, a bishop of the fourth century who was revered for his benevolence. Granted sainthood for the miracles he performed in his lifetime, he is remembered on December 6, the anniversary of his death. One tale of Saint Nicholas recounts his gift of gold to three poor peasant girls. Because their father had no dowries for his three daughters, they were to be sold into slavery. The girls had washed out their stockings and hung them by the fire to dry before going to bed. Saint Nicholas secretly tossed gold coins down the chimney, and they were caught in the stockings. Imagine their delight and wonderment the next morning when they discovered this secret, magical gift that altered their fate and brought joy to their lives.

Immigrants to America from throughout western Europe brought their variations on the legend of the generous Saint Nicholas with them to the New World. Author Washington Irving in 1809 described a jovial old man who rode over the rooftops in a wagon, dropping presents down the chimneys of the houses of good boys and girls. With Clement Clark Moore's embellishments in the classic poem "'Twas the Night Before Christmas," the wagon became a sleigh pulled by reindeer, and the jolly old elf filled stockings that had been carefully hung by the fireplace.

How to make Woolen Stockings

Turn woolen socks into personalized, one-of-a-kind Christmas stockings. Choose trims that complement the homespun look of the stockings. Add patches of flannel or wool fabric, and trims such as buttons, bells, or fringe. For a cuff, simply turn down the top of the sock. Or hand-stitch a fabric cuff to the top of the stocking. Most items can be stitched in place using a darning needle and narrow ribbon, yarn, or pearl cotton.

Materials

- Large woolen sock.
- Cardboard.
- Narrow ribbon, yarn, or pearl cotton; darning needle.
- Ribbon for hanger.
- Embellishments as desired.

1 Insert a cardboard liner, cut slightly larger than the sock, into the sock before decorating with hand stitching; the liner will prevent catching stitches in the back of the sock.

2 Stitch letters, using yarn and backstitches; secure stitches by taking one or two concealed small stitches.

3 Knot a loop of ribbon through top of sock for a hanger. Stuff finished stocking with tissue paper or with polyester fiberfill.

1

2

3

How to make Victorian Stockings

Trim a mantel with unique Victorian Christmas stockings made from elegant fabrics, ornate trims, and tassels. Select fabrics like velvets, moirés, brocades, and tapestries, using matching or contrasting fabric for the stocking cuff. Choose embellishments like lace motifs, ribbons, rhinestones, or antique jewelry. To add body, pad the stockings with polyester fleece or low-loft quilt batting.

Materials

- ⅝ yd. (0.6 m) fabric, for stocking.
- ⅝ yd. (0.6 m) fabric, for lining.
- ⅝ yd. (0.6 m) polyester fleece or low-loft quilt batting.
- ¼ yd. (0.25 m) fabric, for contrasting cuff, if desired.
- ¼ yd. (0.25 m) fusible interfacing, for cuff.
- 4" (10 cm) ribbon or cording, for hanger.
- Lace motifs, ribbons, jewelry, tassels, or rhinestones, for embellishments.

1 Enlarge the half-size stocking pattern on page 62, using a 1" (2.5 cm) grid, such as a gridded cutting board or graph paper.

2 Place fabric right sides together, and cut two stocking pieces from the outer fabric and two from the lining. Also cut two stocking pieces from the fleece or batting. For the stocking cuff, cut one 6" × 15¾" (15 × 40 cm) rectangle each from contrasting fabric, interfacing, and lining. Apply interfacing to the wrong side of the cuff, following the manufacturer's directions.

3 Plan placement of ribbon and other embellishments on cuff; pin or glue-baste in place. Stitch close to edges of trims. *(continued)*

3

How to make Victorian Stockings *(continued)*

4 Baste fleece or batting to wrong sides of stocking pieces. Pin stocking pieces right sides together.

5 Stitch ½" (1.3 cm) seam around stocking, leaving top open. Stitch again next to first row of stitching, within seam allowance. Trim close to stitches. Turn stocking right side out; press lightly.

6 Fold cuff in half crosswise, right sides together. Stitch ½" (1.3 cm) seam; press seam open. Repeat for cuff lining.

7 Pin cuff to cuff lining on lower edge, right sides together, matching the seams. Stitch ½" (1.3 cm) seam around cuff; trim. Press seam toward lining; understitch as shown.

8 Turn cuff lining to inside; press. Baste cuff and cuff lining together at upper edge. Pin cuff to stocking, right sides up; baste at upper edge.

4 **5** **6**

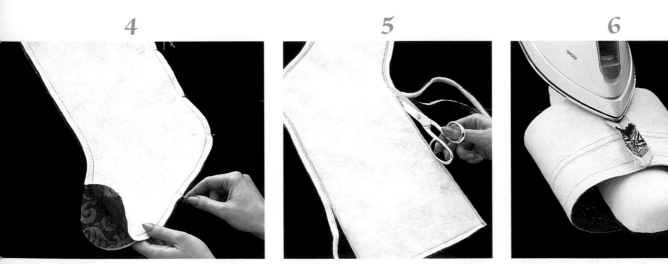

9 Fold ribbon or cording in half for hanger. At back seam, baste hanger and tassel to upper edge on right side of stocking.

10 Pin the lining pieces right sides together. Stitch ½" (1.3 cm) seam around lining, leaving the top open and bottom unstitched for 4" to 6" (10 to 15 cm); stitch again next to first row of stitching, within seam allowance. Trim close to stitches.

11 Place the outer stocking inside lining, right sides together. Pin and stitch around upper edges. Turn right side out through opening in lining.

12 Stitch opening closed. Insert lining into stocking; lightly press upper edge. Hand-stitch lace, jewelry, or other items to stocking, if desired, taking care not to catch lining.

7

8

9

19

The Yule Log

The custom of burning a large yule log is a tradition borrowed from the Nordic festival *Juul*, when great bonfires were lit to honor Thor, the sun god, to tempt the sun's return despite the long, dark days of midwinter. After the Norman invasion of England in 1066, the yule log tradition was passed on to the British, who adopted it as part of their Christmas celebration. On Christmas Eve an enormous log would be brought to the house and placed on the hearth with great ceremony. It would be lit from pieces of the yule log carefully saved from the year before, and it was kept burning from Christmas Eve through Christmas Day. Some believed that ashes left in the fireplace from the yule log protected the house all year from natural disasters.

How to make a Log Carrier

Make a sturdy log carrier to fill with firewood and give as a gift. The log carrier is made from mediumweight to heavyweight fabric, such as upholstery fabric or denim, and lined with cotton duck. The durable wooden dowel handles are easy to grasp, and the bottom gussets prevent twigs and debris from falling out of the carrier.

Materials

- 1¼ yd. (1.15 m) mediumweight to heavyweight fabric, such as upholstery fabric or denim, for outer fabric.
- 1¼ yd. (1.15 m) cotton duck fabric, for lining.
- Two dowels, ¾" (2 cm) diameter, 24" (61 cm) length.

1 Cut large paper rectangle to measure 36½" × 42" (92.8 × 107 cm). Fold rectangle in half lengthwise; fold in half again crosswise, to get a folded rectangle measuring 18¼" × 21" (46.6 × 53.5 cm).

3

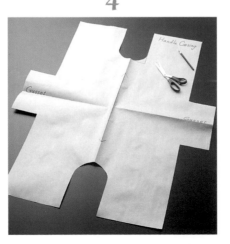

4

6

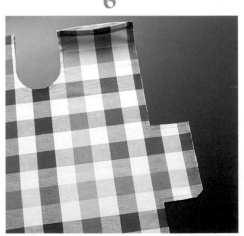

2 Draw a line, 16" (40.5 cm) long, beginning at short cut edges, parallel to and 5" (12.5 cm) away from the long cut edges. Draw a perpendicular line from end of 16" (40.5 cm) line to long cut edges.

3 Draw a line, 9" (23 cm) long, beginning at short cut edges, parallel to and 3" (7.5 cm) away from long fold. Draw a perpendicular line from end of 9" (23 cm) line to long fold. Round the inner corner, using a saucer as shown.

4 Cut on lines through all layers; unfold pattern. Label grainline on long center fold. Label handle casings and gussets as shown.

5 Cut one log carrier piece from the outer fabric and one from the lining. Press under ½" (1.3 cm) on one handle casing of outer fabric; repeat for lining.

6 Pin outer fabric to lining, right sides together, matching the raw edges and pressed folds. Stitch ½" (1.3 cm) from edges, leaving an opening at folds.

7 Trim outer corners diagonally; clip the inner corners to stitches, and clip curves. Press the lining seam allowance toward lining.

8 Turn right side out through the opening; press the seamed edges. Fold 2" (5 cm) to the wrong side on all four handle casings; pin. Stitch close to the seamed edges of three finished casings; stitch again ¼" (6 mm) from the seamed edges. At handle casing with opening, stitch through all layers, close to the folds, closing opening; stitch again ¼" (6 mm) from folds.

9 Pin gusset to side of log carrier, wrong sides together, matching seamed edges. Stitch close to seamed edges, backstitching to secure; stitch again ¼" (6 mm) from seamed edges. Repeat for remaining gusset seams.

10 Paint handles as desired, or stain handles and apply clear acrylic finish; allow to dry. Insert handles into handle casings.

7

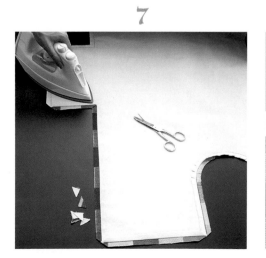

8

9

How to make Pinecone Kindlers

As a befitting gift or seasonal accessory that is both useful and decorative, fill a basket with these paraffin-dipped pinecone kindlers. They burn for up to twenty minutes, while kindling logs for the fire. Paraffin for the pinecone kindlers can be colored red and scented with cinnamon, or colored green and scented with pine, if desired. To light a fire, center a pinecone kindler under stacked firewood and light the wick.

Materials

- Candy thermometer.
- Double boiler.
- Paraffin wax, approximately 1 lb. (450 g) per six pinecones.
- Candle color squares and candle scent squares, one square each per pound (450 g) of paraffin wax.
- Muffin tin.
- Nonstick vegetable oil spray.
- Wax-coated candlewicks, 6" (15 cm) long.
- Pinecones, 2" (5 cm) in diameter or size to fit muffin cups.
- Tongs.

1 Insert candy thermometer into double boiler. Melt 1 lb. (450 g) paraffin wax in top of double boiler over boiling water. Add one square of the candle color and one square of candle scent as desired. Mix gently, using wooden spoon.

2 Spray the muffin cups lightly with nonstick vegetable oil spray. Place one end of wax-coated candlewick in each muffin cup; allow opposite end to hang over side of muffin cup.

3 Cool melted paraffin to about 160°F (70°C). Dip pinecone in paraffin, turning to coat thoroughly. Raise pinecone above wax for a few seconds, allowing paraffin to harden; repeat two or three times. Remove with tongs, and place coated pinecone upright in muffin cup over candlewick.

4 Remove top pan of double boiler containing remaining melted paraffin. Dry outside of pan with towel to prevent water from dripping into muffin cups. Slowly pour ½" (1.3 cm) melted paraffin into each muffin cup at base of pinecone.

5 Allow the kindlers to cool completely. Remove from muffin cups. Arrange in decorative gift basket; prepare note card with instructions for use.

1

3

4

Candles

With the invention of the candle, man could have light whenever it was needed. So, candles were thought to have the power to free man from the terrors of darkness. Throughout medieval Europe, candles were kept burning from December 25 to January 6, a custom originally thought necessary for keeping witches and evil spirits at bay during the darkest days of the year. During Victorian times, candles represented good will for those less fortunate. Candles were placed near windows in many Victorian homes for the twelve days of Christmas as a sign that warmth and shelter could be found there. Today, a candle burning in the window of some Christian homes symbolically lights the way for the holy family, as well as serving as a sign of welcome to guests.

How to make a Molded Beeswax Candle

With their warm, inviting glow and mellow scent, beeswax candles are a year-round favorite decorating accessory. For Christmas entertaining, brighten your table with molded beeswax candles you make yourself. Using innovative products, including flexible polymer candle molds, beeswax pellets, and boiling bags, you can enjoy the art of pouring candles without messing up the kitchen or ruining cookware. Available in many styles and sizes from craft stores or by mail order, flexible polymer molds are durable and easy to use. The beautifully detailed candles can be enjoyed in their natural state or highlighted with acrylic paints, wax-based metallics, or pearlized powders.

Materials

- Beeswax pellets.
- Boiling bag; clothespin.
- Large saucepan; water.
- Flexible polymer candle molds; aerosol mold release.
- Candle wicking, size 2/0; wicking needle or large-eyed darning needle.
- Large metal hairpin.
- Rubber bands.
- Freezer paper.
- Disposable metal pie pan.
- Acrylic paints, wax-based metallics, or pearlized powders; small paintbrush, for embellishing, optional.

1

2

1 Pour beeswax pellets into boiling bag. Roll top down, and secure with clothespin. Submerge in pan of boiling water.

2 Spray inner surface of polymer mold with light layer of mold release. Insert candle wicking into mold, using wicking needle or large-eyed darning needle. Pull wicking taut; secure through large metal hairpin, centered across opening of candle mold.

3 Wrap rubber bands around mold; check seam of mold for proper alignment. Place mold, open end up, on work surface covered with freezer paper.

4 Remove boiling bag from water when wax has melted; towel off any dripping water. Remove clothespin; slowly pour beeswax into candle mold, filling to top.

5 Allow beeswax to cool completely; cooling time may vary from 2 to 6 hours, depending on size of mold. Remove rubber bands; remove candle from mold, pulling wicking into position for the next candle.

6 Cut wicking ½" (1.3 cm) above top of candle. Cut wicking at base of candle, removing hairpin.

7 Heat a disposable metal pie pan on stovetop burner. Press bottom of candle on heated pan; this melts wax on bottom, leveling candle and sealing wick.

8 Embellish candle, if desired, using acrylic paints (snowman), wax-based metallics (angel), or pearlized powders (tree).

4

5

7

8

Luminarias

Among the most beautiful sights of the Christmas season are streets and pathways lined with glowing luminarias. This tradition dates back to 17th-century Spain, when townspeople lit bonfires along the town paths, symbolically lighting the way to Bethlehem for Mary and Joseph. The tradition spread to Mexico and later to the American Southwest, where parades of worshipers walked firelit pathways to church on Christmas Eve. Eventually candles in weighted paper bags took the place of open fires, an idea that may have been inspired by traditional paper Chinese lanterns. In northern climates, luminarias are often fashioned by placing candles in blocks of ice or hollowed-out snowbanks, heightening the candles' glow. Many centuries after that first journey to Bethlehem, rows of flickering lights guide visitors all over the world and welcome them to holiday celebrations and worship services.

How to make Ice Luminarias

In cold-weather climates, ice luminarias add a warm glow to dark winter nights. To create this lighting effect, simply place a candle into a well in a large block of ice. Use ice luminarias to line driveways and walkways. Or add interest to a backyard view by clustering several on a patio or deck. Ice luminarias can be used as long as the temperature remains below the freezing point. Brush the snow off the candles periodically and spray the ice formation with water to return the ice to its clear state. For long-burning luminarias, use pillar candles.

Materials

- Plastic bucket, such as an empty one-gallon ice cream container.
- Empty plastic peanut butter or mayonnaise jar.
- Votive or pillar candle.

1 **Ice cream buckets.** Center jar in the bucket; place rocks in the jar to weight it. Fill the bucket with water, up to the rim of jar. Place the bucket outdoors or in the freezer until the water is frozen. Remove the rocks from the jar.

2 Pour warm water into jar to release it from ice; remove jar.

3 Wrap the bucket with warm, wet towel to release ice from bucket. Place candle into the well in the ice.

4 **Deep buckets.** Fill bucket partway with water; surface of water should be below rim of the bucket a distance greater than height of candle you will use for well in the ice. Freeze water. Complete luminaria, following steps 1 to 3, above, centering jar on top of ice in step 1.

1

3

4

*H*ow to make
Paper Bag Luminarias

Materials

- Mat board or piece of heavy cardboard; mat knife.
- Dark-colored paper bags.
- Cookie cutters or stencils.
- Light-colored paper bags.
- Sand.
- Votive candles.

1 Cut piece of mat board or cardboard so it will fit inside paper bag. The board will protect your work surface and prevent you from cutting through both sides of the bag.

2 Trace designs or words on dark bag using cookie cutters or stencils as templates; trace with a pencil.

3 Insert mat board or cardboard into bag; cut designs out of bags with mat knife.

4 Remove mat board from bag. Insert light bag into dark bag, and unfold. Fill bottom of layered bags with sand; nestle candle in sand in bottom of bag.

5 **Alternate method.** Cut a paper doily slightly larger than cutout design on dark bag. (Edges should not be ragged, because their silhouette may show through bag.) Secure doily to inside of dark bag so that it is centered, using glue stick.

3

5

33

Wassail

Jolly old England originated the rather boisterous custom of wassailing: making merry and drinking toasts to others' good health at Christmastide. Minstrel troupes traveled door to door, singing carols and shouting, *"Waes hael!"* which means "be whole" or "be healthy." Pleased audiences would fill the troupe's empty bowl with hot, spiced ale or wine, a drink which became known as wassail. After a volley of holiday toasts and not a little imbibing, the troupe moved on to the next house.

Wassailing today is slightly more reserved; though seasonal greetings and a warm mug of holiday cheer still go hand in hand. In the spirit of hospitality, friends and neighbors are invited into each other's homes to share good wishes and something warm to drink.

How to make a Scented Coaster

In keeping with the spirit of *"Waes hael,"* these lovely spice-filled, stenciled coasters add soft holiday scents along with your sentiments. Tantalizing aromas filter upward when you place a warm mug on the coaster.

Try different blends of whole cloves, whole allspice, star anise, cinnamon sticks, nutmeg, orange peel, or lemon peel to fill the coasters. Shatter large pieces, like the cinnamon sticks, with pliers. When the fragrances begin to fade, roll a can across the coaster to lightly crush the spices and release fresh scents.

Cutting Directions: Cut six 5½" (14 cm) squares from solid fabric. Cut six 5½" (14 cm) squares from back fabric. Cut six 5½" × 11" (14 × 28 cm) rectangles from polyester fleece.

Materials

- ¼ yd. (0.25 m) solid natural-fiber fabric, for six coaster fronts.
- ¼ yd. (0.25 m) fabric, for six coaster backs.
- ⅓ yd. (0.32 m) polyester fleece.
- Sandpaper, 7" (18 cm) square.
- Masking tape.
- Precut stencil.

- Fabric paints or craft acrylic paints and textile medium.
- Stencil brushes, one for each paint color, or sponge pouncers.
- Disposable plates; paper towel.
- ¾ cup (170 g) assorted spice blend, as desired.

1 **Stenciling on fabric.** Secure sandpaper to hard surface, using tape. Center solid fabric square over sandpaper. Mask areas of stencil, if desired, using tape. Tape stencil in position over fabric. Wrap tape around bristles of stencil brush, ¼" (6 mm) from end.

2 Pour paint puddle onto plate; mix two parts acrylic paint with one part textile medium, if necessary. Dip brush tip into paint. Blot brush on paper towel in a circular motion until bristles are nearly dry.

3 Hold brush perpendicular to fabric, and apply paint in largest part of design, using up-and-down pouncing motion. For shaded effect, apply paint more heavily along stencil edges, leaving centers light. Apply paint to all areas of one color; allow to dry. Apply additional colors. Heat-set paint, following manufacturer's directions.

4 **Alternate method.** Apply dry formula stencil paint, following manufacturer's directions. Use sponge pouncer instead of stencil brush, if desired. *(continued)*

2

3

4

How to make a
Scented Coaster *(continued)*

5 **Sewing the coaster**. Fold fleece in half, forming square. Align back and front of coaster, right sides together; place over fleece. Pin aligned layers together.

6 Stitch ½" (1.3 cm) seam allowance all around, leaving 3" (7.5 cm) opening on one side. Trim corners diagonally; trim fleece close to stitching. Turn; press.

7 Pour ⅛ cup (28 g) spice blend between two fleece layers. Fold seam allowances in; slipstitch opening closed. Topstitch about ⅛" (3 mm) from outer edges.

5

6

How to make Wassail

Ingredients

- Peel of 1 lemon
- 3 slices peeled fresh gingerroot
- 1 stick cinnamon
- 1 teaspoon (5 mL) whole allspice
- 6 cups (1.5 L) dry red wine or cranberry juice
- 6 cups (1.5 L) apple cider
- ½ cup (125 mL) sugar
- 2 oranges, unpeeled, cut into 6 wedges each
- 36 whole cloves

Yield: 12 cups (3L)

1 Place lemon peel, gingerroot, cinnamon, and allspice on a small piece of cheesecloth or in a paper coffee filter. Bundle up the corners and tie top with kitchen string, leaving excess string to hang out of pot for easy retrieval. Set sachet aside.

2 In 6-quart (6 L) Dutch oven, combine wine, apple cider, and sugar. Add sachet. Bring to boil over high heat, stirring until sugar is dissolved. Cover. Reduce heat to medium-low. Simmer for 15 minutes. Remove sachet. Keep wassail warm over low heat.

3 While wassail simmers, stick 3 whole cloves into peel side of each orange wedge. Place one wedge in each serving cup and ladle hot wassail over top. Serve hot.

Silent Night

On December 23, 1818, in the little town of Oberndorf, Austria, Father Josef Möhr attended the town Christmas play. After the play, distracted and unable to sleep, the young priest climbed the mountain overlooking the town to ponder in the dark stillness his dilemma. The following day he was supposed to lead the Christmas Eve service at the village church. Unfortunately, flooding of the river that flowed so near the church had caused the pipe organ to rust, and it had stopped working. How could there be a Christmas Eve service without music?

Back in his room in the wee hours of Christmas Eve morning, with the peaceful beauty of Oberndorf fresh in his mind, Father Möhr recalled a poem which he had written two years earlier. The next morning, he took the poem to Franz Grüber, the organist, and asked him to write a simple tune to accompany the words so that Father Möhr could play it on his guitar. They finished just in time to practice with the choir. That night, at tiny St. Nicholas' Church of Oberndorf, "Stille Nacht! Heilige Nacht!" was performed for the first time.

Just by chance, the master organ builder who eventually came to repair the organ heard the carol and copied it. In his travels he passed it along to others, including some families of traveling folk singers. Eventually "Silent Night" became one of the most beloved carols and was sung all over Europe and America, though no one knew of its origin. It wasn't until 1854 that Franz Grüber learned of its fame and came forward to say he had composed the tune. Father Möhr had died in 1848, but Grüber still had his original poem.

The Christmas Tree

The fir tree was revered long before the birth of Christ because, while other trees seemingly died in winter, it remained green and alive. Late in the Middle Ages, Germans and Scandinavians brought small evergreen trees inside their homes in winter to show their hope for the coming of spring. The decoration of trees at Christmastime has its roots in German traditions. The German religious leader, Martin Luther, is said to have seen a fir tree illuminated with sparkling stars while walking through the woods one Christmas Eve night. He was inspired to bring home a small fir tree to his family and light it with candles. Another German, Prince Albert, brought the tradition of a lighted and decorated tree to England when he married Queen Victoria, whose tastes influenced much of the traditions and decorations we now associate with the holiday.

By the early 20th century, the custom of decorating a Christmas tree was adopted by most Americans of European descent. Small evergreens were decorated with candles, sweets, ribbons, dried flowers, and even small gifts. These elaborately bedecked trees were kept hidden from children until Christmas Day, as children were told Santa brought the tree and its trimmings in his sleigh.

How to make a Wire-Mesh Bow Tree Topper

For an elegant-looking tree topper, create a large wire-mesh bow from aluminum window screening. The window screening, available in shiny silver and dull charcoal gray, may be left unfinished or painted gold, brass, or copper. The bow also may be sprayed with aerosol glitter for added sparkle.

Cutting Directions: Cut the following from window screening, cutting along the mesh weave: one 8" × 38" (20.5 × 96.5 cm) piece for the loops, one 8" × 28" (20.5 × 71 cm) piece for the streamers, and one 2½" × 7" (6.5 × 18 cm) rectangle for the center strip.

1

2

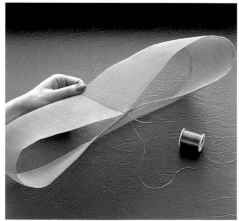

Materials

- Aluminum window screening.
- 24-gauge or 26-gauge craft wire.
- Utility scissors.
- Aerosol acrylic paint in metallic finish, optional.
- Aerosol glitter, optional.

1 Paint both sides of each rectangle, if desired; allow to dry. Fold up ½" (1.3 cm) on long edges, using a straight-edge as a guide. Fold up ½" (1.3 cm) along short edges of streamers and one short edge of center strip.

2 Cut 16" (40.5 cm) length of wire. Form a loop from rectangle for loops, overlapping the short ends about ¾" (2 cm) at center. Insert wire at one overlapped edge; twist wire to secure, leaving 2" (5 cm) tail.

3 Stitch through the center of overlapped mesh with long end of wire, taking 1" to 1½" (2.5 to 3.8 cm)

stitches. Pull up wire firmly to gather mesh; wrap wire around center, and twist the ends together; trim the excess.

4 Hand-pleat width of streamer at the center; place below the gathered loop. Wrap length of wire around the center of loop and streamers; twist ends together. Paint wire to match bow, if necessary.

5 Wrap center strip around the bow, concealing the wire. Stitch ends together with length of wire. Apply aerosol glitter, if desired. Secure a length of wire to the back of center strip for securing bow to tree.

3

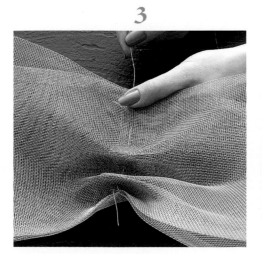

4

5

Poinsettias

According to legend, long ago in a small Mexican village lived a young girl named Maria and her little brother Pablo. Though they were very poor, they always looked forward to Christmas, when there were many parades and parties in the village. At the village church, a large manger scene was set up, and it was the custom on Christmas Eve to bring gifts for the church to the manger. Maria and Pablo had no earthly possessions to give to the Baby Jesus, so on their way to church one Christmas Eve, they picked some weeds that grew along the roadside. As they placed the green plants around the manger, the other children teased and taunted them for their foolish gesture. But to everyone's amazement, the top leaves of the plants turned to bright crimson stars and filled the scene with stunning beauty. To this day, this native Mexican plant, called "flame leaf" or "flower of the Holy Night," is a symbol of Christmas.

In America this plant is called the poinsettia. It was named after Dr. Joel Poinsett, the first American ambassador to Mexico and an avid botanist, who first brought it to America in 1828. Poinsettia plants are given as gifts and brought into our homes in early December. Their beauty remains throughout the season and, in many areas, can be planted outdoors to grow through the summer. The blossom of the poinsettia is actually a group of small yellow flowers in the center of a ring of red, white, or pink leaves at the end of a branch.

How to embroider a Poinsettia Design

The delicate beauty of silk-ribbon embroidery can be used to embellish purchased or sewn linens for special table decorations. Embroider poinsettias using the deceptively easy Japanese ribbon stitch. Make a series of French knots to form the centers of the blossoms.

Materials

- 7 mm green silk ribbon.
- 7 mm white, rose, or red silk ribbon.
- 4 mm gold silk ribbon.
- Chenille needle, size 20, 22, or 24.

Tips for Silk-Ribbon Embroidery

1 Thread chenille needle with a length of ribbon no longer than 18" (46 cm) to avoid excessive abrasion. Prevent ribbon from falling off needle by threading needle and taking a stitch through ribbon near one end.

2 Leave 3" (7.5 cm) tail on underside of cloth. Pierce tail with needle as first stitch is pulled to underside. Pierce tail again with second and third stitches. Clip tail close to last secure point.

3 Secure ribbon end by slipping needle under two stitches on underside. Wrap ribbon back over stitches, piercing twice through ribbon. Hand-tack tail with matching thread. Clip tail close to last secure point.

4 Use an awl to make a hole in closely woven or heavy linens so wider ribbons can be easily pulled to other side of cloth without damage.

1   **2**   **3**   **4**

How to embroider a Poinsettia Design

1 **Japanese ribbon stitch.** Bring needle up from underside. Smooth ribbon flat in direction of stitch. Insert needle at end of stitch, piercing center of ribbon. Pull needle through to underside of fabric until ribbon curls at tip; take care not to pull ribbon too tight.

2 **French knot.** Bring needle up from underside. Holding the needle parallel to fabric near the exit point, wrap ribbon once or twice around needle, taking care to keep ribbon smooth.

3 Insert needle very close to exit point, holding ribbon in place close to wrapped needle. Hold ribbon while pulling needle through to underside of fabric, releasing ribbon as it disappears. Ribbon forms soft knot.

1

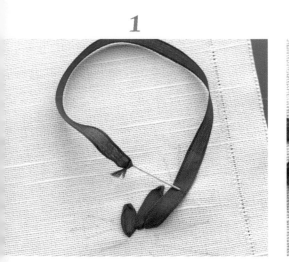

2

3

Advent Calendar

The coming of Christmas is a time of great anticipation, especially for children. In German Protestant households in the 19th century, the twenty-four days before Christmas were marked off with a chalk line, one day at a time. This was done to count off the days of Advent, which in Latin means "coming towards." The first printed Advent calendar, produced in 1908, was a series of twenty-four little pictures that could be glued to cardboard to mark the days. Soon after, calendars were produced that had little windows to open, which usually revealed Bible verses. The idea caught on and became very popular until the beginning of World War II, when cardboard was rationed, calendars with pictures were forbidden, and the tradition was lost for a time. After the war, in 1946, the tradition was rekindled and many Advent calendar styles are now commercially produced in all parts of the world. Many families mark the passing of each day in December with a special calendar saved from year to year.

How to make an Advent Calendar Wreath

This Advent calendar wreath provides a unique way to share the joy of expectation all season long. Decorate a natural or artificial wreath, and open one small gift each day as you count down to Christmas.

Purchase small, plain envelopes in stationery stores, or make your own envelopes using decorative or holiday wrapping papers. Number an envelope for each day; use a decorative pen, or select letter transfer sheets from assorted styles available at art and stationery stores.

Into the daily envelopes, slip coupons that may be exchanged immediately or throughout the coming year. Consider a small treat, a special privilege, or a day off from a specific chore; design them to please your family. Or purchase small, flat gifts, such as foil-wrapped candy coins or charms.

Materials

- Wreath, 36" (91.5 cm) in diameter.
- Clusters of small embellishments or berry stems.
- Paddle floral wire; wire cutter.
- One to three large ornaments.
- Small embellishments, such as berries.
- 1 yd. (0.95 m) ribbon, 3" (7.5 cm) wide.
- 7¾ yds. (7.1 m) ribbon, ¼" to ½" (6 mm to 1.3 cm) wide.
- Twenty-five envelopes, 2" (5 cm) square, or decorative papers to make envelopes.
- Decorative pen or transfer letters, ½" (1.3 cm) tall, and stylus or craft stick.
- Glue stick; paper punch.
- Twenty-five coupons or small flat gifts.

1

2

3

1 Secure clustered embellishments to wreath frame at center top, using floral wire; bend stems or secure more clusters to follow upper curve of wreath. Allow an unadorned arc to remain bare at bottom; arrange needles to partially cover floral stems, if used.

2 Suspend large ornaments at center top, using narrow ribbon. Secure small embellishments as desired.

3 Tie bow in wide ribbon. Secure bow to wreath, just above ornaments, using wire; arrange and trim tails as desired. Cut narrow ribbon into twenty-five 11" (28 cm) lengths. Secure ribbons randomly over wreath surface, using wire; allow at least 2" (5 cm) between ribbons. If using purchased envelopes, omit step 4.

4 Cut 4¼" × 3¼" (10.8 × 8.2 cm) rectangle from decorative paper. Mark foldlines on wrong side of paper, 1" (2.5 cm) from one short side and 1¼"

(3.2 cm) from other short side, ⅞" (2.2 cm) from top and ⅜" (1 cm) from bottom. Score foldlines, using table knife, if paper is heavy. Cut out four corners; shape flaps slightly, as shown. Fold envelope; secure narrow side over wide side and bottom flap over sides, using glue stick. Repeat to make twenty-five envelopes.

5 Label envelopes with numbers 1 through 25, using decorative pen. Or position transfer sheet over each envelope, placing number near envelope center; rub number, using stylus or craft stick. Gently lift transfer sheet to ensure complete transfer.

6 Punch hole at tops of envelopes, using paper punch. Insert coupon or small flat gift in each envelope. Tie envelopes to wreath, using ribbons; arrange numbers randomly to avoid lopsided arrangement as envelopes are removed. Hang wreath, using wire loop on back.

4

5

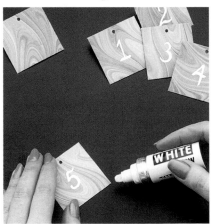

6

Candy Canes

Sweet confections have long been a part of the Christmas celebration, though the candy cane may be one of the most popular and easily recognized. The origin and symbolism of the humble candy cane is somewhat a mystery because it seems to have been created simply as a sweet treat for children that later was given symbolic attributes. All stories seem to agree that the candy cane began as a straight stick of white candy that was tied to Christmas tree branches along with other treats and trinkets. One tale from the 17th century suggests that the choirmaster of the Cologne Cathedral in Cologne, Germany, bent the white sticks of candy into the shape of a shepherd's staff and gave them to children to keep them occupied during Christmas Eve services. It wasn't until early in the 20th century that a candy maker in Indiana attributed the white color to the purity of Jesus and added the red stripes in remembrance of His sacrifice and death.

Christmas Cards

Now a seasonal mainstay, Christmas cards were born from procrastination and innovation. While correspondence at the holidays was already a tradition by the middle of the 19th century, a Sir Henry Cole in England is thought to have sent the very first card for a Christmas greeting. Because he was behind in his holiday writing, he asked a friend, artist John Calcott Horsley, to design a suitable card. Within a few days he had produced a small drawing, copied by lithograph, hand colored, and mounted on pasteboard. It depicted a family raising wine glasses in toast to the season, with the sentiment, "A Merry Christmas and a Happy New Year to You." Other artists began to follow suit, and because Queen Victoria loved the idea and sent Christmas cards of her own, it soon became quite fashionable. By 1860 Christmas cards were being mass-produced and the industry began to flourish. Though countless styles can be purchased, many people prefer to show extra thoughtfulness by designing their own Christmas cards.

Holiday Cookies

Cookies, in some shape or form, have been around since the beginning of recorded history, born of the need for portable food with a long shelf life. During the Middle Ages, bakers in the Middle East used eggs, butter, and cream to lighten flour paste morsels, then added fruit and honey to make them more tasty. The word "cookie" comes from the Dutch word *koekje,* which means "small cake." It was the Pennsylvania Dutch who first introduced holiday cookies to America.

Cookies have been part of celebrations long before the first Christmas. Germans baked their anise-flavored *springerle* and the Scottish their shortbread for the pagan winter solstice celebrations. After Pope Julius declared December 25 as Christmas in 350 A.D., Christians adopted cookie baking as part of the Christmas celebration. Many of the Christmas cookie recipes we bake today originated in the European countries centuries ago; each carries with it generations of folklore and tradition.

Stocking Pattern

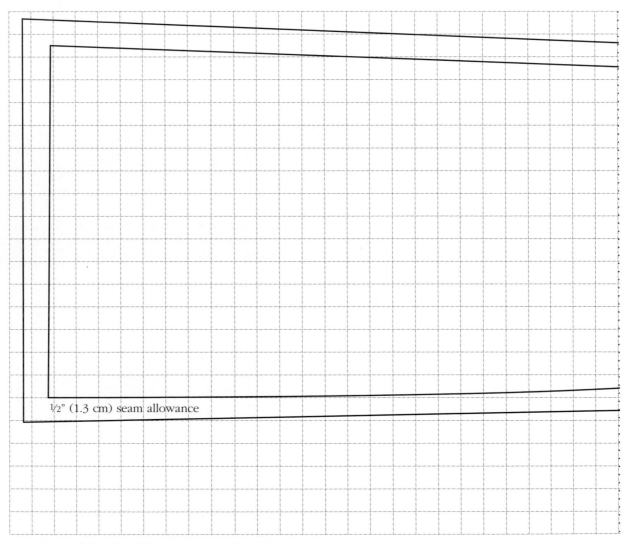

½" (1.3 cm) seam allowance

1 square equals ½" (1.3 cm)

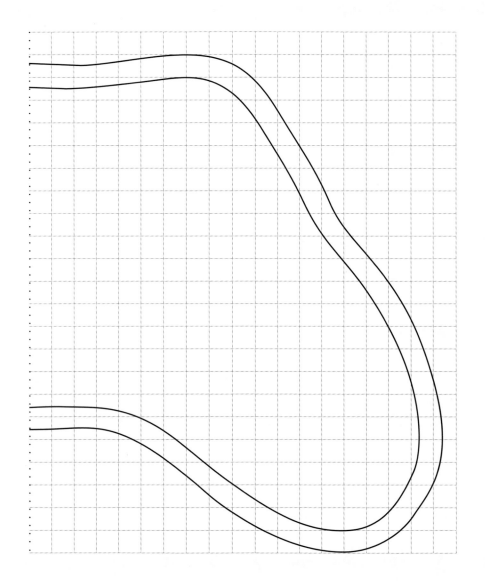